BALANCING

POETIC MOTIVATION

DEBBIE GRAVETT

Balancing

Cover design by Apple Pie Graphics – www.applepiegraphics.co.za
Interior illustrations by Kamryn Nelson
Stepping stones illustration by Patrick J Nel
Interior design by Debbie Gravett

First Edition Printed March 2026

Paperback 978-1-0492-5253-7
Ebook 978-1-0492-5254-4

www.debbiegravett.co.za

For Bruce, Jordynn, and Harley,

Thank you for having more faith
in me than I did,
and all your encouragement.

To the rest of my cheerleaders,

I am forever grateful
for your follow-ups, and for listening
to a dream which took a while
to come true.

Love you madly!

Dear Reader,

I give you these words,
don't ask me what they mean,
because they are yours
to interpret as you please.
No wrong or right
in your translation,
read them as you must,
and decide how they fit.
I'll be glad if they touch you,
find meaning in your midst,
for these words were writ
expressly for you,
with great heart's intention,
for you to feel each one.

WHAT'S INSIDE

Balancing It All

Canoe down river,
obstacles in equilibrium,
precarious balance
over the rapids of life.
Another challenge
added to the pile
at an obscure angle.
To hold in place,
avoiding a swim,
in icy waters of pain.
Remove one at a time
using a counterweight,
providing support
to keep it all dry.

Contrary Conversation

Through fog, mist, haze and rain,
the poor falling of money,
how do I offer hope or motivation,
when I blindly feel for it myself?
Easier to see reflections of gloom,
take part in such conversations,
add sludge to the insatiable swamp.

Oh, to be bold, take the contrary view,
find sunshine and pretty rainbows,
not in fantasy's realm, but tangible form,
exert the effort, whatever it takes,
oppose temptation of the shadowed path,
choose jagged stones instead of worn cobbles,
shine light to warm the dispiriting fog away.

Being

Whistle of crystal air
Creating a tune
For fire to dance
In flicking tongues
For water to flow
In a babbling brook
For earth to turn
Her beautiful majesty
Breath to move
Calm and effortlessly
I am a vital part
In this symphony
Of undeniable belief
In infinite possibility

My Reason

Born of purpose
Fault lines like Earth
Woven into the fabric
Weft of innate gifts
Unique pattern of being
Only mine to voice
Only mine to complete
I give the world
The gold in my veins
Because
This is my place
This is my time
And I belong

Sweet Mirror

Gossamer wisps of cotton candy,
your love melts onto my tongue,
adding delectable sweetness to life.
You are my reflection,
and I am sugar.

Sunnyside Up

You kiss my temple oh so gentle,
warm the crown of my head,
descend through my undulating chest
until you reach my extremities.
Tingle and stir to blissful awakening,
your golden rays coax me
to leave the comfort of my bed.
Folded in brilliant light,
granted energy for the coming hours,
even on days you do not shine,
hope still hovers above the clouds
if I should choose to feel its heat,
to heal the chills within my bones,
you are always available to me.

Repeat After Me

To the one in the mirror
who frowns back at me
with scathing disdain,
a loathing so deep.
Today I promise
not to disparage you,
instead,
encourage and support.
Today I promise
to love you with all my ability,
because I will remain
in all the breaths of your life,
reminding you
of the magic that lives
inside the beauty of your soul.
I love this reflection,
in all angles of being.

Not Broken

A slip isn't a break
Broken isn't done
It isn't over
You are still the one
To waft your essence
Be your greatness
Come back to life
There is no lateness
Exactly where to be
Unlikely as it seemed
To make your life
What you've dreamed
Or better

Blowing a Spark to Life

In the inhospitable landscape of thought
I scale the charred cliffs of hope,
my demeanour blackened by soot and ash.
A desolate place my psyche has come to,
but even in the hell of my mind, I can strive
to resuscitate my dehydrated dreams,
by shaking off the burnt bits of thinking,
extinguishing the infernos of fear
that spark, raging out of control,
and coaxing calm embers of potentiality.
Flickering in the shadows,
ignite the brilliant sun to illuminate
over lush green meadows of growth,
beside gushing turquoise waters,
where I can shimmer and gain ground.

Ubuntu

I am because you are

The hand of a stranger coming from nowhere
When you fall off the edge of a sheer cliff

Skip through your front door to a beautiful day
A welcoming world of infinite kindness

Choose to believe it
And choose to be the same

Still Breathing

Do I need a reason other than breath
To lift my weary body from slumber
Forget the myriad of excuses
That lie on the tip of my tongue
To give life a hard pass
Before the day has even begun
Pushed under
Way too many a torrid time
Beneath the bumpy rapids I navigate
I'll continue to lie on this rushing river
Stare at the stunning blue sky
Because I'm still breathing
And sometimes...
I j.u.s.t n.e.e.d to take a breath

SEE Yourself

Silver glitter sparkles in her hair
Magical mischief plays on her lips
Amazing and beautiful reflection
Only visible once I decided
To see her there

Nature's Red Carpet

Clock of songbirds
to wake a peaceful night,
ray of morning dusts a brow,
scent of fresh, reviving air
fills hungry lungs,
whispers of butterfly beauty
visit coffee's aromatic sip,
strength of the tall, mighty oak
gives fortitude.
Welcome to your day,
venture forth into the unlimited.

Already Done

Unfurl, uncurl,
rolled in a ball
will not get you there,
though it shuts out the night,
hides you from the light
of all you wish not to see.

Unfurl, uncurl,
there is life to be lived,
living to be done,
and none is so bad
that it can't be achieved.
Look at what you've already done.

New Moon Letter Burning

To fire and lack of light
Send intentions, oh dear Night
Written on this piece of paper
Thoughts transmitted like vapour
Embers float to a wishing star
Manifestations unbar
Waiting with faithful belief
For their realisations relief

T.o.u.c.h.i.n.g Ground

(Palindrome – mirror poem)

Bare feet touching Earth,
buried in russet and walnut soil,
flexible and movable,
sturdy tether to the ground.
Quelling loose floating feelings,
unhinged amongst the clouds,
d i s c o n n e c t e d from life,

lost in a confused state of mind.

Breathing in calm, crystal air... no longer
lost in a confused state of mind,
disconnected from life,
unhinged amongst the clouds.
Quelling loose floating feelings,
but sturdy tether to the ground,
flexible and movable,
buried in russet and walnut soil,
bare feet touching Earth.

Let’s Not Pretend to Live

Earth turn,
moon rise,
sun set,
sun rise.
Every day,
and every year,
life’s mimicry,
mimicry,
does not have to be so.
Choose your adventure,
spin your own wheel,
stop when you must,
try anticlockwise.

Planning by Sight

Breathe in,
breathe out,
inhale,
exhale,
you've got this day,
it lies before you.
Plan a good one,
expect great fun,
see it be,
envisage the detail.
Rise,
and enjoy its honesty.

Troubles Away

I've come to Mother Earth asking,
to ground my sensibilities,
to know I am tethered to her centre,
safe to release all that troubles me,
to her great transmuting ability.
The grey smoke and black sludge
that impedes my progress,
converting the jagged rocks
dragging in the pit of my gut,
and those weighing on my shoulders,
to priceless gemstones of energy,
of love, protection, and guidance.
Of all that will help me along,
to walk a little straighter and lighter,
and know this day is won.

What Are You Sharing?

Misery does not love company,
don't seek it out, nor share it,
don't wear it on yourself,
nor ask it of another.
Wish it on its merry way,
and replace it with a smile,
even if a novice at pretending,
keep it there until it sticks.
Find little things to give it reason,
allow the joy to multiply,
and share it with your neighbours.

Truly Celebrate

Whatever your celebration,
menorah, red string, or mistletoe,
balloons, rings, love, or green things,
first breath, or last,
from the west coast to the east,
the north to the south,
under full moon or new,
immerse yourself
in all that it means to your heart,
and be blessed.

Tell Them, and Do

Tell the ones you love,
near or far,
past or present,
spread the energy.
Never assume
they must know
the contents of your heart.
Remind them often,
in case they ever wonder
if it's changed.
Spread love consciously,
receive it abundantly.
Let them not be
three mere words
falling casually
from your lips haphazardly,
let them also be
what you do.

Natural Occurrences

Life is the ebb and flow of a tidal wave,
to knock, and dip, and rise again,
peaks, valleys, and occasional chasm,
the graph and course of living.
Attitude allows the triumph of
the depth and length of the valley,
sheer drop to the walls of the abyss,
to allow the mountaintop view,
and the glory of the summit.

Time

Exact season for beautiful bloom,
no clock should tick in the garden,
each petal unfolding perfectly
without comparison to their neighbour,
and the same should be allowed for you.

Ride the Horse

Don't wait for the steed
bearing your saviour,
carrying solutions
to all that ails you.
Climb on the horse
you find in the barn,
pick up the lance,
and fight your battles.
Then ride into the sunset
knowing you're saved,
problems solved
by your own deft hand.

Up to You

Acceptable to not be okay,
unacceptable to wallow,
your actions will raise you,
to be okay tomorrow.

As You Are

Too amazing to melt into
someone else's mould,
wax your own flow.

It is Okay

It is okay to be okay.
Don’t search the garbage
for all the challenges
you have discarded,
past their sell-by dates,
expired,
and dead.
Their duty done,
no need to hold on.
It is okay to be okay.

What Comes Naturally

Have you ever heard anything so absurd,
as monkeys trying to pull up trees,
and elephants trying to climb them?
Denying nature's natural gifted ability,
failure looms large in their attempt,
no sign of their capabilities,
just the choice of their pursuit.

Remember Them

Gaze to the stars on the whisper of wind,
take dreams to the moon and present them,
to the enchanting glow of her magical pool,
travel by beautiful moonbeam or cloud.
Dance across meadows and climb tall trees,
play with Mother Nature in her forest of wishes,
with dandelion messengers and sunflower gleams,
enjoy a childhood of many wondrous possibilities.
Where all has potential to be something great,
of magic and mystery, and out of this world.
Sticks become wands, pumpkins become chariots,
now gaze to the stars and rediscover your dreams.

Allow It

Let me hold your shattering pieces,
whatever the reason let it be,
allow progression through the stages,
for healing is found in each of these.
And when the season is right,
and rains have been and gone,
sprouts will shoot for this charred heart,
green, beautiful, and healthy.

You Fit

Stand up,
stand up,
stand tall.
Puzzle of the world,
has a glaring gap,
and you're the perfect fit.
In every decision and situation,
stand up,
stand up,
stand tall.
Your place is right,
air, wind, fire and water,
all where you belong.

Doing It
(Acrostic)

Squeezing great effort
Trying something
Obliterated by failure
Painful, shamed attempt

Turn your back
Rejection of this view
Yell from the rooftops
In defence of the battle
Now own up to the doing
Give credit to your action

Enjoy Your Day

Tomorrow is two steps up,
today stands level before you,
offering many a gift at your door,
like the middle child quietly begging,
not to be stepped over and ignored.
Requests not to go down to yesterday,
rather pay it fair dues,
in its wonderful offerings,
see and believe, they are for you.
This step holds the greatness needed,
crafted and waiting,
and for declarations of gratitude
it endeavours to give more.
So, enjoy this day that is given,
let it be yours,
do not postpone for later
the magical delights of today.

Compared to What

Apples and oranges
The fruits of despair
But don't pay attention
To the differences there
Only failings in compare
Those picked too soon
Are bitter and sour
Those growing too quick
Fail to fill with flavour
In the glorious orchard
Fragrant with perfection
Of wafting ripeness
You too will season
Just right

What haunts you?

Ghosty, Ghosty,
come out and play,
I'll gift you to the wind,
release the claws
I've sunk into you,
declaring ownership.
A past mistake
redressed as experience,
a right old blessing.
I'll face your haunting,
process the feelings,
wish you well,
for it is time
I moved on without you.

Manifest Joy

Natural resting place
In euphoric endless flow
Riding the rainbow of bliss
Vivid dream of an ideal life
Animated into tangibility
Never doubt the possibility
Accept it as probability

Simply Ask

Shoulders round for burdens to slip,
troubles to fall to the ground,
but if they shouldn't,
all you need do is ask.
The wind and the fire,
the earth and the rain,
the being up above,
the Universe all around,
whomever you feel called to speak to,
an answer you'll get,
perhaps not the shape you're expecting,
but exactly the form you are needing.

Time for Repair

Slow release from her grasp,
reluctantly untangle yourself
from the comforting embrace.
Be parted for a little while
to allow feet grounding connection,
take confident, conscious steps,
to follow waking dreams,
sculpt, adjust and create a life
of a fervent heart's desire.
But she will always be in the wings
to replenish the tools you use,
the mind, the body, and the soul,
to achieve these many things.
Remember to cuddle her
like in the healing arms of love
—Sleep will be there for you.

It Can Be Done

By read of these words is knowledge,
by sight and sound of this verse is ability,
by the breath to suck them in is life,
and all deserve our gratitude.
For hope, opportunity, and the dawn they bring,
they announce their intention to greatness,
the anthem by which your morning begins,
for you are able in all things,
if not to do, then to learn,
or find assistance in that of your wish.
All can be done.

A Better Reply

Look to your heart,
look to your soul,
mine are not answers,
for you are the key,
to all your questions.
Within you they live,
so, listen carefully,
without agenda
to adjust the truth,
or stubbornness
to ignore the whispers
if they vibrate differently
to what you desire.

Bring Wishes to Life

Laughter and freedom,
dreams and wishes,
a thousand white diamonds
to the blue sky.
Lighter than feathers,
but just as soft,
by my intention,
and whispered breath,
I release them thus
from their anchored stem
to the moon and stars,
to find footing in life,
in palpable form
believe them to truth.

In Time

Thankful for this waking day,
no matter the longitude or latitude,
find vital tools in its bountiful promise,
to tackle challenges and blessings,
receive that which is meant,
and forge a road most perfect.
Furious drive of great desire
yielded by life's tempered speed,
despair not the plan of the Universe.
Do not whisper a desperate wish
to inattentive gusts of howling wind,
but...
converse the hearts deepest dreams
with faith and trust released,
in patience see what needs
become reality.

You’ve Done it Before

When hope no longer shares your waking breath,
when substance is your chosen anaesthetic,
when all is bleak and filled with gloom,
recall life’s ebbs and flows of past.
Remember misery seeks company,
and do not provide it a friend.
Flash back to battles of then,
acknowledge your standing presence,
reason to believe you’ll win again,
stronger, wiser, sharper and surer.
Have faith, not in the world that holds you,
but in your own abilities and beyond.

Good Morning

Sun, burn the haze of sleep that captures me,
wind, awake the spirit that hibernates within me,
water, wash the sadness from my face,
earth, ground my feet for this rebirth.
Let me rise from fiendish nightmares
and stand tall in the light of this new day.

Shining Back

Look only for the comforting light,
know it, because you knew the night.
Be that light, and cast across the earth,
invigorating the energy of another's worth.
Toss a smile or kind word to the fray
and brighten this beautiful day,
being the match struck for their joy,
flames of love you must deploy.
Singe their hearts with your smile,
without subterfuge nor guile,
but bask in the wondrous side-effects,
the reflected joy kindness projects.

The Whispers

Listen to the voices,
hear them speak,
their tune in harmony
with your heart,
the bell's ring
in melody with intuition.
Then heed their words,
and act upon them -
reach out to a friend,
take that walk,
dance in the rain,
or sing that song,
for there are angels
guiding you.
So listen,
and let them.

Meditated Mind

I dispense of worries on my breath
From top to toe, I clean them out
In the quiet of closed eyes
I clear the cobwebs, dust, and shadows
Blow these murky lurkers from my body
I inhale air to rounded shoulders
Release the load that lies there upon
To the greyness of my exhalation
For the wind to hurry it away
To the ground these charred skeletons must fall
And I rise
With less weighted thought than before
To breathe clearly, the light that hid behind
The darkness clouding my fearful mind

Know What You Know

Fairies and lightning bolts,
the war of goblins and gnomes,
a certainty your heart knows,
not that which others say.
Cement foundation,
step with both feet,
firmly into your knowing,
be anchored not swayed.
Let them speak whatever they may,
for their words do not make truth,
only believing them does.
It's all supposition,
tainted opinion from the outside.
Stand firm in the midst of the war,
but do not join the pointless fight,
the wonder of an open, honest heart
needs no defence to be its proof.

You Sparkle

Violet sparkling soul of royalty
Twinkling jewel of the day and night
Effervescent gem of immeasurable worth
You are the magic that shines
With a birthright to majesty and greatness
To a life of wonder and brilliance
Believe in the quality of you
And all you humbly deserve

Old Sadness

Lift your head,
bowing creates a double chin,
sadness draws crow's feet
around vacant eyes,
folds around a beautiful mouth,
meant to shine and smile
touch the gorgeous curve of a rainbow.
So do your facial exercises,
pulling funny faces,
showing warmth to strangers,
these all to give a youthful glow.

Find Your Life Circle

All that burns is not ash,
for ash is food for the soil,
the soil is an anchor for us,
and the cycle and circle turn.
Follow the arcs and bends,
let the flames burn,
cauterise or singe,
search for the warmth
or the birthday candles.
Find the wheel that turns it,
perfect for you.

The Accountant

Your count has not been tallied
Your books have not been closed
Life is here before you to counter debts
You have time to adjust
Right up to your last and final audit
Life's balance sheet has room for correction
Should anything be vastly out of line
Remember, you are the accountant
Who creates the entries in this book
And when the double lines are drawn
May you be proud of the balance taken forward
From this life to the next
Carry in your soul the account you have kept
No hiding from the taxes due
For the way you have lived
But red need not remain
Unless you're quitting now
If you want to be in the black
Before your time is up
Then make your mark a good one
Of kindness, empathy, and love
For the world will remember that
And you will take it with when you go

This is You

In your millionth apology
for the very same sin,
realise that this is you.
Own it or change it,
but don't apologise again.

Give it to Nature

Come with me to the clearing
Take my hand and let us go
To the greenest, softest grass
Waiting to take us in
To welcome us with open flowers
Nodding heads at our decision
Bare our feet to the earth
Ground our energies in her sand and rock
Trust her dependable, firm support
Give her our sad and tarnished woes
Under the daylight sun and midnight moon
In the sweetest, freshest air
To breathe our biggest dreams and wishes
Among the leaves and branches tall
Let them rise to the heavens transmuted
To twinkle as our goalposts

Gifts of Our Own

Does it matter who did it first?
Does it matter who can and who can't?
Why must I be better or worse?
I exist in my own being,
where actions are mine to claim,
without influence or competition.
Look only at me and what I do,
no reason to judge by comparison,
see me and my unique moves,
let them speak for themselves,
because I wasn't born
to best my fellow man.
The aim and goal I have,
to be better than yesterday,
be more of who I am.
The fish who can't climb a tree,
the gorilla who can't or won't swim.

In the Full Moonlight

By the light of the moon
Fill me up and make me strong
By the light of the golden glowing moon
Recharge my energy and renew me
Clean me of the dust and the drudge
Let me shine once more as I am meant
To reflect her beauty and brilliance
In the light of the moon
I am whole again

Not Up to You

I'm sorry—not really,
if you think you have a say,
but this life is mine,
and I'm meant to live it my way.

Got This

The world is out there
But I am in here
Strong enough
Grit and guts
No matter the outside
Forging ahead
Always enough

I Am the Pilot

Take me on a journey to the land of happiness,
let me board the flight to get me there,
to know only joy and ringing laughter.
But this departure does not exist,
It is I myself, who will fly me to that destination,
for it exists in the wings of my chest.

My...

Don't do it, just don't
Don't put that word before any negativity
Don't claim it
It isn't YOURS
Let it pass through
If it must touch you at all
An experience you need to feel
But labelling grants it permanence
So just don't
Never
Not at all
Unless it is something you wish to keep
Then by all means
Call it YOURS
Make it YOURS
All those good things in life
Because that's what YOU deserve

Lost?

I thought I wandered from my fated path
A detour on a road that was not there
Over rocks, gravel and uneven surfaces
I thought I was lost for a time
Deep in the darkness of the damp forest
Hidden by giant oaks and firs of stature
Who loaned me trunks to lean on
As I borrowed strength from them
Took a rest to release the necessary
To gather myself, and discover myself
I thought I wandered from my fated path
But all these painful experiences
Were part of my intended journey
No mistakes or missteps, just building blocks

Earth Deposit

Lay my wars to rest on the ground,
give them to the worms for food,
that my soul may digest peace.

The View

My world is filled with magic and miracles,
angels and fairies and great possibility,
with kindness, compassion, and giddy joy.
Beauty in tall trees and crystal-clear streams,
the gentle caress of a warm, loving sun,
milky, enchanting light of a guiding moon.
My world is filled with love and understanding,
tolerance and embrace for all that is,
with a love that reaches my soul,
greatness and opportunity in abundance,
bathed in the glow of eternal illuminated hope.
What I choose to see returns to me.

In Nature's Arms

Trailing fingers in diamond river reflect,
to throw my grief like rocks into the stream,
that jagged edges might be smoothed,
nervous energy brushed with gentle leaves,
to calm the torrent of raging blood
roaring and flooding my ears.
Return to bird song, and soft breeze,
return to the rustling trees.
Tender wave across my ruddy cheeks
attempt to blow them dry.
I, too hopelessly lost in my melancholy
to appreciate the healing of Earth's hand,
with outstretched arms to comfort,
always ready to receive me.
No matter my state of distress,
to impart energy of grace,
and breath of tranquillity.
Transfigure my sorrows into hopes,
remind me of forgotten dreams,
to restore the memory of my beautiful soul,
lift me to my feet with encouragement,
to try repeatedly.

Hear This!

Hey you!
The one who reads these words today,
I feel I need to tell you this in all earnest,
so, could you stop and really listen.
Please take heed of what I say,
for these come from my heart,
and you need to hear them,
every single syllable.

Don't beg them to stay,
Don't change for their whim,
YOU are enough just as you are.

This is Me
(Shaped Poem)

Own it!
Who you are!
The beautiful soul
That questions things
Wonders about themselves
And tries desperately to grow
To be a better version of
Yesterday's reflection
In the mirror of
Judgment
That you
Check
Often

I
Own
It

Peace

You will not find me in a whiskey barrel,
nor in the whispered gossip about others.
You will not find me in drugs, food,
or any addictions,
but in the silence of breathing,
and the paused rest between,
in the beauty of sweet Mother Nature,
and the value of self-belief.
There you will find me in abundance.
There you will find me for sure.

The Picture We Paint

Sunshine and rainbows,
daffodils and honey,
enough rain
to quench your thirst,
friends and family
to love you,
and an abundance
of self-worth.
Now open your eyes,
and feel it so.

When It's Too Much

If the day is overcast,
look through the clouds to beauty.
If the news isn't what you want,
turn up your favourite music.
If the world feels upside down,
find the ones you love.
When it all gets a bit too much,
have no guilt in resting.

Rolling Tides

Fractured by breaking waves,
paddle under them,
through them,
dig deep.
Hold your breath,
floating waters will come.

Getting Up is Hard

Rip me from my mourning bed,
claws of sunlight challenging,
spilling in, to invade my covers,
its clutches on my sadness
blinding.
Shred this misery of mistakes,
wanting to stay right here,
not rise and face the day,
for it is not the life I dreamed of,
nothing like.
But now's the time to change that,
or embrace it,
find a reason to raise my head,
with dappled hope peeking.

Float With It

The running man,
whose toes only skim the ground
occasionally.
Untethered to life,
floating like a balloon lost to the sky,
without a string to be caught
nor attached to stability.
Unsure,
at the mercy of the gust,
directionless and impotent.
Have faith
in the lungs of the Universe.

Not On Your Own

Let them love the fibres of your being,
the stitches that keep you together.
Allow them to patch your worn threads,
repair the holes that might appear,
but before you give the task to others,
take up the needle and thread,
but *never* believe it is the only way.
The world grants helpers and friends,
and you help them,
by allowing their kindness,
and in turn, we're all aiding one another.

Where Do We Find It?

Our value doesn't lie in their eyes
Neither does it come from their mouths
It lies in our own beating heart
In the respect we show in self-speak
Our value
Our worth
Lies within us

• • • • • ♥ • • • • •

Scattered Pieces

Sledgehammer to the rock
Splinters like dandelions to the wind
I will not collect my broken pieces
Scattered far and wide
For they are who I was
And now I build myself anew
I shall not gather nor search
For the faults of my past
Nor my failings
Because from now
I am who I build

Faith in the Weeds

I can't tell you I'm standing in a field of daisies,
when in truth I am amongst the nettles,
hooked on thorns and lost in brambles,
stung and downright trapped in a challenged mind.
But I can sniff the air for a heavenly scent
of dozens of bright scarlet roses,
seek minuscule, narrow slivers of warm sunshine,
and with all my heart believe,
a clear path will find me here.
While I wait in faith to be within the beauty,
dream of these possibilities.

Your Glow

Intangible sparkle
Today's magic
Illusive to a camera
Only heart captured
May you feel it
In the core of your being
May it shine from you
And through you
Light your day brightly

Focus Here First

Only tend to the land
Where my feet strike
Leave my footprints light
May this be the way of the world
For Earth's beauty to be right
And in turn, to humanity
The same kindness shown
Imagine this peace in delight

Making Your Day

Good morning.
Hot beverage in one hand,
these words in the other,
now let us begin.
See this day,
hold it up to the light,
let the panic list be eclipsed,
caged lungs lifted by a soft breeze,
leave the frantic ticking
drowned out by birdsong.
These precious hours
gliding through storms,
bones rested at ease.
Go to sleep
with this day as yours.
Good night.

Eyes Wide Open

Like injured layers of skin,
my eyes grow new,
with the more I learn.
The way I see changes,
I grow,
the wider my eyes open,
the deeper I see within.

Polished Beauty

Let the world be your oyster
Your safe space with a little friction
That is polishing you up
To be the most glorious pearl you are
A blessing to the world
Let the world be your oyster
Feel safe and glow

Let's Cause a Wave

Please tell me today,
how can I make you smile,
because I desperately want it,
I have a fever for this desire,
for you to have joy on your face,
and deep in your heart.
So please tell me how
I can see happiness in your eyes.
See me smiling at you,
and let's see if you can do it too.
Let us cause a ripple of lips,
turning upward to the sky.

Sanctuary

When the world has disappointed me
Humanity, shown me its ugly side
I seek the sanctity of your gentle arms
The soft landing in your lush lap
I draw strength from your core
Ground and balance my spiralling mind
In your solid, silent energy
Harmonious melody you give my soul
Shaded in the boughs of your peace
Protected and supported
Even in the chaos of your healing
I nestle into you
My favourite hiding place
In Mother Nature's arms, among her trees

Feel Your Feelings

(Villanelle)

Embrace the chemical disruptors that run
Triggering complexities of existence
Do not hide them from the brilliant sun

Pumped from the centre of a heart undone
Tears trickle against denied resistance
Embrace the chemical disruptors that run

Though those of darkest blue hold a gun
Discuss them to reduce their insistence
Do not hide them from the brilliant sun

Silent secret murmurings weighted tonne
Release their mystery to defy persistence
Embrace the chemical disruptors that run

Gushing warm endorphins intricately spun
Dance and joy a public subsistence
Do not hide them from the brilliant sun

Wade through discomforts until there are none
Do not value hidden, unspoken inconsistence
Embrace the chemical disruptors that run
Do not hide them from the brilliant sun

Leave it To the Universe

Silken flow of fabric in the breeze,
easily wrapping magic in the air,
receiving the legacy of synchronicity,
everything falling into place.
Notes of harmony in your symphony
delight at the conduct of the Universe,
in infinite wisdom to your needs,
plays the melody of your strings masterfully.
In tune and time, wiser than you,
to float on the wave of chance,
enjoy this planned life of happenstance.

Missed Moments

What do I do every day?
Unconsciously breathing in and out,
I rise, I eat, I work, I eat, I travel, I eat,
vegetate and sleep.
I glance behind me at time,
take it in my hands, inspect it,
trying to change it, improve it.

I turn and look ahead,
imagining it, living it, feeling the future,
vividly painting exact plans.
I haven't looked down, and again,
moments have gone,
to stand behind me, to be past,
and I've missed more of the now.

Make Magic

Let yourself not be subdued,
your passion not crushed nor destroyed,
be wild, be free, and share your words,
show me your talents, so varied and great.
Let them sing, let them shout,
paint the lands and the skies,
be loud with your actions,
be proud of who you are,
for we all have something to share,
a contribution to make.
Let no one take this away from you,
quiet or not, let me see,
the brightness of the magic you make.

I Decide

Chameleon of my environment,
do I wear the draining colours of drama,
or the energising shine of joy?

Your Moments

There are moments in life,
moments that protect you,
moments that direct you.
Every moment has meaning,
every moment is special.
This life doesn't have
infinite moments in it.
To capture and keep,
to fill with memories,
decisions to be made,
actions to take,
words to be said.
There are moments in life.
live them all,
live them well,
for you don't know
how many moments you have.

Make Time

Time has no replacement
Its value knows no bounds
Discovered only when it's gone
Sleep replenished with it
Memories made with it
Loved ones lost with it
Healing takes place with it
Tick tock, time is passing
What will you make of it?

Surrounding Light

I do not recognise myself
in the person they describe.
I see my deep-seated negativity,
all my glaring mistakes,
my faults and failures
on my fingertips to list,
protest on my tongue.
They, on the other hand
feel the need to specify,
all the good and beautiful.
The mirror and I see the shadows,
the ones who love me see the light.
For them I am most grateful,
for now I see the Yin and the Yang,
and gravitate towards the light.

Master Craftsman

Potter of your life,
take hold of the clay,
wet hands of creation
craft as you may.
Wrong movement
never a mistake.
Much learned in
straying from the
original design,
starting over
always an option,
adding colour too.
Still with the same clay,
masterpiece created
daily,
by hands belonging to you.

No Expectations

With all things, voice your expectations
For one cannot fail if they never knew the goal
But should you have no expectations
May you be the recipient of wonderful surprises
When more than you could ever hope for
Is delivered with a smile.

I Come First

Loving what I do
Loving who I am
It's important
It's necessary
In search of happiness
I found this truth
Along the way
Loving me
Was loving you
Caring for me
Was caring for you
Nobody wins
If I don't come first

Healing

When my heart lies in pieces,
my confidence beneath it,
all in tatters on the hard floor,
cold lancing into my marrow,
my core beyond warming,
light of hope a distant recollection.
I look to nature's beautiful example,
when her surface is charred,
tears and time bring green shoots
to heal her blackened scars,
and mine fade too.

Faith in What I Feel

The eyes of my soul see the invisible
Know the unknowable
And all I need do
Is trust in these, and myself

Intention Please?

Voice choked by my own hands,
ten fingers lay across my throat,
self-inflicted silent screams I squeeze,
cries for a merciful release.
Fear of asinine or insufficient words,
keeps them tightly sealed within,
judgment from outside and in,
gatekeeper of my vocal cords,
until I can hold the lock no more.
Burgeoning ideas slipping from my lips,
touching lives and souls with effect,
for they are honest from my core,
with only gentle, loving intent.

Your Mark

He melted in the moonlight
to the Earth where he belongs,
took the troubles of the day
and filed them in the soil.
He rose by the dawn
from the Earth where he belongs,
stamped the world with his mark,
decisive in his being.

Here Now, on Point

(Shaped Poem)

I control
just the pinpoint I
stand on, like a ballerina's
pirouette, in this vast eternal
Universe. I do it to the best of my
ability, remembering that I only lead
myself, my actions and reactions,
the magical power that I yield,
which I offer to the world
in the most beautiful
authenticity.

Taken Care Of

Fantastical imaginings
Of permanent peace unknown
Calm brush of a gentle breeze
Waved into every cell of my soul
Fear and anxiety outfoxed
By trust in great power
Myself, and the Universe
No need to know tomorrow's fortune
Because every today is taken care of
And so too am I
Always!

You are the Music

Add your drum beat to the rhythm of the world
Let your unique vibration enhance the sound
Do not stay silent for the comfort of others
Your tune is meant to be heard.

Put Me First

Pick me up and put me first
You've thrown me to the floor
Too many times to count
Stomped on me as if to prove
My great lack of Earthly worth

Pick me up and put me first
The reason you were put on Earth
To build me up and let me grow
Please listen to me mirrored face
Time for respect above all others

Pick me up and put me first

Here's Another Day

Aromas of the morning
stretch to reach me,
rouse me from my cosy cocoon.
Birds offer a welcome choir
for me to greet the day.
Twenty-four hours to use,
offering the promise of another
fabulously beautiful day.

Seeing Through the Grey

(Shaped poem – D for Debbie)

Take a journey with me
From the easel to the canvas
Find my soul between raindrops
A blur, with no lines of black and white
But smudges of grey keeping it all unclear
I think I spot sunshine between the clouds
Sparkle of hope, before casting off once again
To locate my purpose and my place on the soil
Or could it be that I belonged in water all along
Denied it for fear of being rejected as different
Could I sail rough seas of challenge and not sink
Because my soul already feels like it's drowning
Forcefully shoved off the end of the pier by life
Is it a test of my ability to swim, or a lesson
Because the Universe wants me to succeed
Offers light at regular intervals as proof
All I need do is open my eyes to see
The beautiful painting through
The colours of the storm

What Your Day Will Be

When it is quiet,
before the buzz begins,
see the day ahead,
the best you can wish.
Sky the colour of your happiness,
music speaking joy to your soul,
enough breath to invigorate your core,
and energy to tackle anything.
Gratitude for the great and small,
a day that delivers all you need.
See it, be it, believe it,
live it,
trusting each minute
as yours.

Dirty Window

The window is dirty,
sparse putty in the pane,
a blurry view of life,
waiting for a cleaner
to make it all clear.

A choice to be had:

squint through the filth
and wait,
or
lift a rag.

Riding Waves

Beyond the debris of the day
Lies prime possibility
Above the pounding waves
Twinkling stars or the warm sun
Beneath over-powering thunder
Bubbles of air holding hope
To surface back into the light
To float in caressing warmth
Or in magical moonlight
A bounty of options and choices
To meet the next glorious wave

Finding a Lighthouse

Crystal bubble of breath
Glistening in water
Threatening to steal my air
Gasping in the overwhelm of life
I look to your light in my darkness
Beacon of hope
To respire calmly once more
Bobbing on the ebb and flow

Your Move

Rooster's crow and dawn's glow
Or alarm calling and traffic honking
Find yourself where you wish
Or play the game of chess
One gradual motion at a time
To move to your bliss

Undergoing Maintenance

The world is askew,
missing its pulse,
mountains have tilted,
rivers run dry.
Arrhythmic vibrations
in the centre of your core,
no light in your aura,
no hope on your face.
Still the earth keeps turning,
the sun and moon rising,
equilibrium to be found
in the knowledge of repair.

A leaf from Nature's Book

Like autumn leaves falling,
losing the oranges, reds,
and yellows of your life.
Not disintegrating,
but preparing
for regeneration.
Not broken and bare,
but resting and healing,
ready to bloom and flourish,
revitalised and stronger,
with no fail in the time taken.

Short Seasons

Frozen on winter's floor
No life to be had in the cold
Surrendered to the barren and bare
Pain is the only source of warmth
Even that will become numb
But this too shall thaw
A season of life preparing for beauty
A season of life getting ready for growth
A season of life that is but a melting icicle

Don’t Doubt Yours

(Cinquain)

If each
Single sand grain
Would doubt its worth, soil would
Yield to the wind, and the world would
Vanish.

In Front of You

Lap of the ocean
Crash of the wave
Waft of the wind
In a heart so brave
To tackle each day
Wake and rise
Wash shadows away
March to the beat
See faces in clouds
Smiling at you
The horizon to aim for
Opportunities en route

May I Have this Dance?

When the world is making a noise
Listen to the music within
No need for a partner
Take yourself for a spin
Whirl your inner child around
Let the silly, the innocent, and wild
Lift your feet off the ground
Without a care for the audience
Feel the freedom of being yourself
Then introduce them to that

Add Curves to Your Heartbeat

It's one of those days I know.
Lately, there have been many,
each flowing into the next,
no border nor rest,
no hope nor light.
The tone of the drone
is monotonous,
survival is unaccompanied,
no action-movie soundtrack,
but with a desperate clinging,
like a fading heartbeat,
waiting for the silence
of mundane existence,
until the end,
with a screaming flat-line,
marking the release.
But before that day is served,
throw in some curves,
waves of pleasure,
say yes to adventure,
or simply a night out,
to bring meaning
to that final melody.

No Action Necessary

The world is a symphony
Let Mother Earth play for you
Deserving of her show
You never need do anything
Your birthright to hear her sing
To find beauty and wonder
Be happy and enjoy

New Beginning

(Haiku)

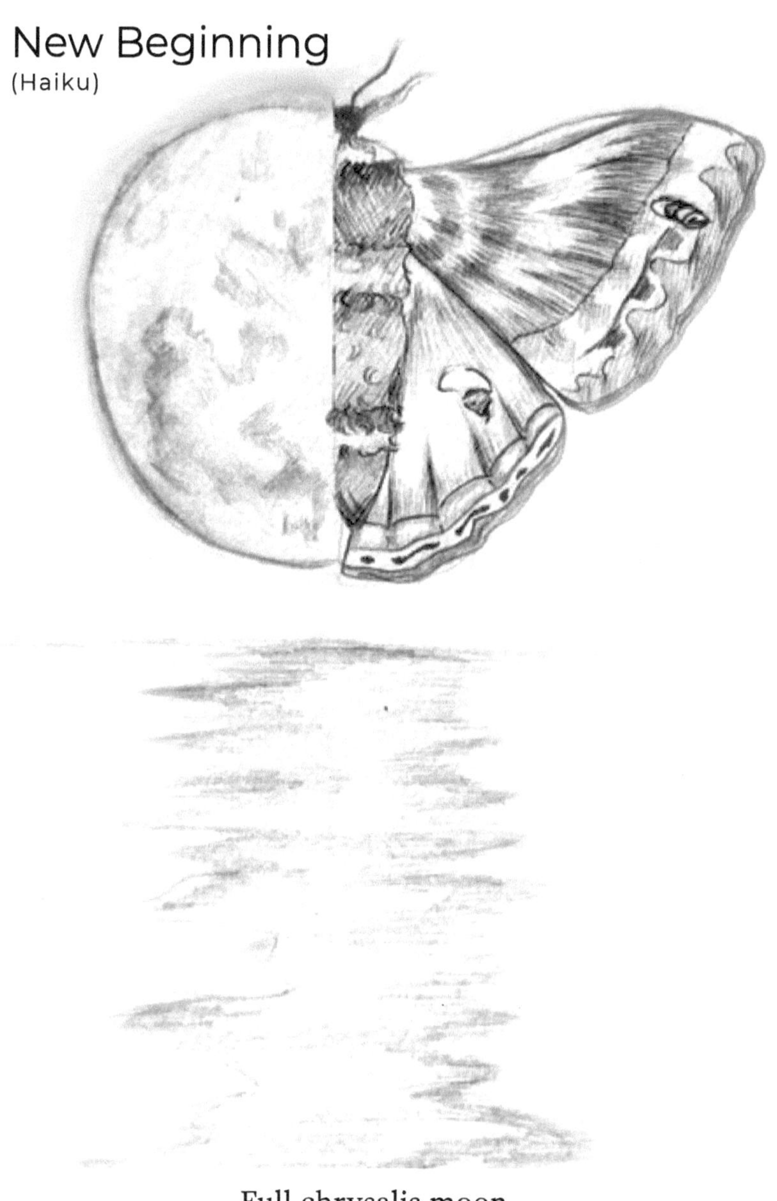

Full chrysalis moon
Birth me anew from darkness
Into fresh waters

The Light Inside

Shimmer, shine, mirror of mine
Show me your secrets
Reveal your true face
Shimmer, shine, mirror of mine
Drop the wretched mask
See me in my scars and lines
Shimmer, shine, mirror of mine
Let me out of this reflection
From the silver to physicality
Shimmer, shine, mirror of mine
To not repeat my melancholic memory
But learn from your example
Shimmer, shine, from this body of mine

Energy for the Soul

I open myself up to healing
By the power of the moon
And the strength of the sun
I am well

The Final Say

Toss an opinion or suggestion
Like pebbles at my window
But do not break the glass
For I must live in the house I build
And will not allow your hands
To force these breathing walls

Skip the Tune

Don't let that record stick,
negative scratches on vinyl,
reiterated repeatedly,
dug in deep,
digging dark holes,
that transform into belief.
If it reverberates,
and does not resonate,
chuck it out,
find another song,
that sings a refrain
to make your soul dance.

Spectacular Day

Let magic be the first to mind
Infinite horizon envisioned
Beyond the border of Earth's end
Greatness beyond human eyes
Have faith from the marrow of bones
Belief from the heart of the soul
That today is phenomenal
In every shape, form, and kind

How I think of You

In the salt of my tears, find minerals
In the blisters on my hands, love
In every thought of me, a return call
In my memories, diamonds of us

More to life

Crumbs off the table,
birds scavenging on leftovers,
or the ant, while grasshopper rests,
working to live and scrape by,
barely so, living on air,
a dull stare into oblivion.
Filling the empty glass
with a hole in the bottom,
but do nonetheless,
for there is more, please believe,
we all have purpose here.

Through Impossible

On the cold, grey concrete road
Cavernous cracks create tears in the surface
The mind tumbles into the abyss of disaster
Scratched and scarred by sharp edges

Then pushed from the chasm of despair
By fledgling green shoots of assistance
Struggling through the wounds of impossible
To sprout new branches of promise

Chimes Ringing in Dreams

Bells knocking by fingers of a breeze
Feathered across their cold metal curves
Tinkle harmonious tune of tranquillity
In halftime metronome, subdue the rush
To breathe
To think
To be
Filling the vast landscape of the soul
With fantastical intention rung to reality
Imagination played to actuality
From dreams, wishes, fairies, and dragonflies
Heart's content sung in magical melody
Brushing our blushing cheeks in the sun
Taking a moment

I am Guided

By the sight of angels,
and the footsteps of guides,
I travel my journey in life.
Trusting their vision for me,
asking for help when in doubt.
By the sight of angels, I see,
and the footsteps of guides,
I grow.

Outstaying the Storm

The wind whispered,
“Come away with me,”
a tempting thought.
Leave troubles behind,
begin again,
free as the breeze,
light as air.
But it too turns to storms,
blowing like a hurricane,
a tornado’s chaos,
and a pouring monsoon.
So I stay,
face, and conquer
the challenges I have,
finding joy in the triumph.

The Timing

The hands of the Divine clock
Tick to their own chime
No matter my desperation
All is exactly as it is meant
And I can only find peace
In accepting what is
What will be

Hold the Roots

Bring me the moon and I'll show you her magic
Lasso the sun, and I will make you warm
Bring me the rain, and I'll teach you to dance
All lessons I am still learning from
Show me a tree, bare of a single leaf
I'll hug it and speak of the skies to pursue
A plant with no flower to colour the world
I'll tell you of its many green shades
There will always be shears to cut it down
But I'd like to be fertile soil to hold the roots
To keep it up and see it grow some more

Come Out to Play

Capture the child
The essence of magic
No boundaries to dreams
A canvas of the Universe
Limitless imaginings
Capture the child
And infuse me
With magical beliefs
I've lost along the way
All is possible
A wand can be waved
Let go of the nay
Only say yes
Believe it into being
A plastic tub is a sailing ship
Few twigs and sheets, a mansion
Capture the child
And be it

There are Refills

When the flowers are dead
The party is had
The friends have left
It is all over with
Alone in the dark
Everything past
There are memories
More fun to be had
Plans to be made
Joy to feel
For it is an infinite cup
You must allow to refill

Critical Burn

Today I wrote a letter for myself,
I had to have it down in words,
not to keep and read again, but to burn.
Release these feelings I have bundled up,
remind myself of achievements, big and small,
nullify the list of failures, that truly aren't a thing,
for I have judged myself by other's standards.
With the goal of healing freedom I did imbue,
folded to three corners: body, mind and soul,
watched it smoulder, die, relight it times a few.
The Universe made certain I was ready to let go,
disintegrate the picture I have skewed,
took to heart my magic in its burning orange,
reminded of my exceptionality, great where I am.
So, if you're on the turntable of self-recrimination,
take a breath and put your pen to paper,
write some words, a line or plenty.
Remind yourself mistakes are lessons,
nothing to regret or grieve.
Give to you the pass you give to others,
to be human, changing what you wish,
fly free from ashes of your own critical opinion,
and celebrate your wins.

Not Only Dreams and Wishes

Feather-light dandelions are fine
to set your wishes upon,
whispered to the Universe
to bring the words to truth.
But get out of bed,
get dressed,
set your mind to the ready
with faith and unyielding belief.
You shall receive the best meant,
take the action you need.

Travel Mates

The landscape of life is not to be traversed alone,
offered many companions to help on your way,
ethereal, physical, invisible and tangible,
guides, angels, friends and family.
Yours to pick your travelling partners,
the ones you wish to stick,
those who support and encourage,
lift you up and wish to see you at your best,
for that is what you deserve.

The Necessity of Sleep

They meet you in the dream hours,
sanity, recovery and repair,
behind the curtains of closed eyes,
they patch the panels of your brain,
clean unnecessary debris from your files,
reorganise, catalogue, and throw to waste
the obsolete and inconsequential.

They meet you in the dream hours,
so don't leave them waiting,
because clutter will build up in memories,
a fog will settle on your thoughts,
and function will begin to diminish.
Keep your nightly appointments,
for they are there to help.

Bubble Boundary

Blow breath to the bubble surrounding you
to protect your essence and energy,
increase the ambit of its security.
Deny the well-established tradition
to bow to whim or want of others,
forgetting what you yearn and crave.
Within this magical bubble confine,
keep interfering intentions out,
to fathom your worth and being,
lay down boundaries of acceptance,
with the new strength of self-respect.

Surrender the Care

Come dance with me in the breeze
Let your soul loose in the motions
Close your eyes to the rest of the world

Come dance with me in the sea
Let yourself float in the crystal-cool spray
Close your eyes to the rest of the world

Come dance with me among the trees
Let your limbs wave as the branches do
Close your eyes to the rest of the world

Come dance with me under the marquee
Let your body flow to the feel of the music
Open your eyes to the rest of the world

Continue to move without care

Nobody Owns Me

I do not belong to anyone
I belong here on Earth
I am not a possession
I am possessed by my soul

An Inspiring Change

Your rising light
Your changing hue
Great wonder you doth imbue
You're treading right

A meandering path trod
This is not a life-sentence
Will without repentance
Veer where you wish to plod

Walking the Fearful Line

I walk the line like a drunkard test
Focused on the very narrow
Rigid and inflexible to prospects
Hunched tightly into myself
I do not take in all of life
Breathing shallow
Nor see the bigger picture
Where much more could be mine
For I allow fear to block it out

Gatekeeper

Catch the words that trip across your tongue,
examine them before they leak.
Will they make the world better or less?
Once evaluated, release or disregard.
Not only with the spoken should you practise,
dissect your thoughts the same.
Let them be, to make you stronger, surer,
builder, not destructor and destroyer.
Be as kind to yourself as you would another,
even kinder still.

Not a Fantasy

Moon drops sparkle in his eyes
Fairy dust twinkles in his hair
He brought hope and magic
Back from his visualised fantasy
Excitement vibrates in the air
Because he believes its reality

Seeing the Flaws

Mirror, mirror, I see myself in you
Not a carbon copy reflection
Of eyes and teeth and hair
But in that which irritates me
Once I thought it was only you
But I have dug to discover
You are a trigger for what's inside
Now that I know this
I work to uncover the reason why
To better understand
Is my first step to improve

Through the Cracks

Flower blooming from the paving crack,
how do you constantly push through?
Such inhospitable clime you've picked,
yet you poke on out and blossom,
unfold to the glorious day, or to the rain.
I long to know the secret of your pain,
for I am ready to quit at meeting a pebble,
shrivel up, never sprout above the ground.
But seeing you gives inspiration to overcome,
seek fractures of opportunity in challenges,
for I know they do exist,
by the vibrant yellow of your petal's shine.

Helping Hands

Has your hand reached out this week?
Stretched it to the furthest distance,
to the one who shies away.
Has your hand reached out this week?
To the one who likely needs it most,
but does not wish to be a burden.
Has your hand reached out this week?
Because when you help without reward,
the world offers hands back to help you too.

Unlabelled

A bottle without a label
My contents undefined
I am...
Who I decide to be
The actions I take
An unlabelled entity
Of beauty and magic
I am...
What I say I am

From today onward
I will not sideswipe at myself
Waiting for the bottle to break
I will polish it, cherish it
And allow the ingredients
To build and burst forth
Writing my own tag

Not One Flower

Seeds planted in my brain
I pull weeds of discourse
That have grown too sturdy
Watered with concentration
Focus spreading their roots
Anchored and compounded
With more affecting comments sown
I find unfathomable reason to prove
But still I fight to uproot the invasive
For I am not this flower nor that
I am a bouquet of many
A complex cross-pollination
Of unique magnificence
Not mere words said by others

Pick Your List

Your list of failures in your mind
Your achievements unlisted
Though you might not think it so
Take time to write them out
Perhaps it will take a moment
To shift your focus and find some
No matter the size, do not judge them
Pen them in their glory done
Read the one that lights you up
Spurs you on and reminds you
You have done great things
And there are many more
Waiting to be added

It Takes Differences

The bird sings,
the monkey climbs,
the fish swims,
and you too,
have a talent
that makes this
beautiful world
work.

Multiply Happiness

Don’t invite me to your sadness,
don’t visit me in mine,
but come and share in joy,
allow for blissful time.
Don’t own the negativity,
don’t label it as mine,
release it to the birds above,
give joy a chance to smile.

Chemical Symbiosis

Magic potion of the Earth
in exact perfect formula,
only with your essence
does it work.
Continue to add energy
as it lights the life of others,
who can't possibly tell you
how precisely you should be.
Active ingredient of another smile,
the chemistry of adding success.
Please continue to be the catalyst.

What Did I Say

Was it wrong, what I said yesterday?
Did I offend or possibly be misunderstood?
Each word rolled around in my head,
turned back again, and again.
Judged exquisite flower, succulent strawberry,
or putrid odour of last month's potatoes,
weeping foul from grey furry eyes.
It is by this examination that I learn
to clear my internal cupboards each night by bed,
wake in the morn to set new intentions forth,
and make them rightly so
in each action of the day,
to wonder no more
at the content of what I've said.

In Times of Trouble

My fingers fumble in the aura of departing hope
Grazed tips gaining purchase to pull her back
The stench of desperation leaking from my pores
Afraid to be lost to the darkness once more
I remember the beauty of the moon in the night
Knowing it is here where I can find my inner light

Built by Obstacle Courses

The clouds hang heavy,
a marsh of difficulties multiplied,
dragging legs through thick, oozing mud,
rot and decay depressing the senses.
But clean water waits at the end
to wash the curves of these muscles,
defined and toned by strugglc,
trained to conquer and complete
the journey that remains.

What Are You Looking For?

I couldn't see you through my misery,
though you were right next to me,
nothing existed but my next breath,
and the decision whether to take it,
the fog and darkness blinding.
I couldn't see you through my challenges,
only focused on the thought of more.
But when I found a persistent spot of light,
started thinking about sunshine,
the weather changed in front of me,
I could only see the brightness of your smile,
because now that was all I was looking for.

When Deciding

In choice of what to do, ask this:
Does it make you laugh?
Does it make you smile?
Does it lift your heart up high?
If so, do that,
if not, examine another.

Out of Air

Breathe
A simple thing
That needs reminding often
When the wind is stolen
From our soul
        ... Breathe
When the air is knocked
Clean out of our lungs
        ... Breathe
When the world is crushing
Our bodies last oxygen molecules
        ... Breathe
Simple, but sometimes impossible
Breathe in clear blue clarity
Breathe out grey shadows
Inhale
Exhale
Repeat

I Have Decided

Grounded, stern, and stubborn
I dig my heels into the earth
Decision made
I will not be swayed
Today I will, without a doubt
Remove my surly pout
No matter what comes my way
I will have
A wondrous and glorious day

In the Background

In the engine of a car
I know not how it all works,
I do not understand the detail,
but know it gets me there.
So too does the Universe,
grinding gears in the background
where I do not see them,
for the best of life to find my road,
I follow this belief.

Have a Great Day

Whether it's sunshine
Or gloomy grey sky
Thunderstorms or
Warm summer days
Feel the wind
Or the sun
Or the drifts of snow
Or the driving rain
Have a good one

Regret or Recalibrate

Walked a path to a different destination
Dreams and plans of youth taken deviations
I could ponder melancholy on the outcome
But none would change the current location
Only from the next raised foot can I turn it
Left, right, or continue straight forward
There is no one hundred-and-eighty
Nor steps of rapid rewind
Standing still another choice
But time will not, and so I must decide
Or fear return to certain melancholy
A little further down the line.

Seeing the Beauty

The lateness of the hour
The softness of the moon
I could complain I am awake
But why destroy
The beauty of the view

What I Can Do

The clocks are ticking backwards
The past is running forwards
I can't keep up with the tortoise
But I beat the cheetah in a race
The world is upside down and inside out
Understanding needs a forehead scratch
Though I'm tempted to reach far beyond
In a desperate endeavour to set it right
There is but only one thing I can do
Control the thoughts and reactions I allow
To run through my head and down my arms
And exit my body into the world

The Bigger Picture

Please do not get lost in the darkness of details,
laser-focused on trivial errors
that all greatness and beauty fades to a blur,
for there is much more to fill the living pixels
than this dismal vision.
Step back and see all the glory there is,
more wonder waiting to be seen
beyond the frame you have set.

All in Good Time

The river finds its way
And so too will we
Sometimes cutting long
Through the granite
Others rushing through

Chip Away

The boulder of today
List of conquering Everest
Get a chisel and a hammer
Write down the tasks to be done
Continuously strike the rock
Chip away each little stone
Until the boulder lies in pieces
Cementing a path beneath you

Joy of Health

Picture of beauty
Smile on your face
Picture of magic
Happiness beaming
From eyes aglow
Originating
From a heart beating
At the perfect pace
And so may it be

Don't Worry Tomorrow

Around the corner,
down the road,
there waits a surprise.
Fear it, anticipate it,
look forward to it,
none will change its shape.

High on Life

The needle of euphoria
Is not what I wake up to
A glass of amber liquid
Not to brush my teeth
An up-sized burger, chips
And gassy soda
Will not fill the holes
Buried inside of me
Temporary solutions
Problems will outlast
Requiring constant refill
With more than the last
An addiction to life
The high that I ask
Only allowing a hit
From happiness
That is unsurpassed

Too Great to Compare

Do not compare to anything
Nor reach for another's star
For you are unique perfection
Exactly who you truly are

Discover your own magic
Beyond the summer's rose
Remove the mask of envy
To reveal your natural pose

Shine Your Light

The
stars and
moon shine
in the darkest night sky
on the roughest of seas
you are someone's
lighthouse

Not Always Light – That's Okay

Light is black and dark is white
Bed by day and bed by night
I am left and not quite right
And that is well within my sight
My shades tinted in various greys
My vision is gloomy for days
Nothing is wrong, it's all quite right
Everyone needs a day of night

Wished on a Dandelion Seed

Dandelion seed landed on me
Am I somebody's greatest wish
Did they blow their fate to me

Dandelion seed landed on me
I'm want to believe I am the wish
Somebody made on that seed

Dandelion seed landed on me
Fly back and let them know
Wishes do come true

For them, and for me

Reflection of Love

Have you told them you love them,
those beautiful eyes in the mirror?
Have you done something
to show them it is true?

FOR You

Morning has dawned,
eyes have opened,
prospect twinkles
from every moment.
Pluck dandelions,
and blow three wishes,
let them float,
without setting chase,
but do what you can,
in their endeavour.
Trust your support,
and all serendipity,
wanting to see,
life happen FOR you.

Sizing it Up

Small is the mouse in your house
The pimple on your face
Small is the bump in your road
The dent in your wallet
But small is never
The size of your dreams

My Precious Life

Ball of string to unravel
Little kitten at play
Carefree and curious

Boisterous cat adventuring
How long is this piece of string?
Nobody knows

Adult feline purr
Clawing at hectic knots
But knit it together

Add to the blanket of earth
Proud contributor
To the patchwork quilt

Adding to Your Life

I could travel alone,
but where is the joy in that?
Time on my own,
crucial
to restore my balance,
allow me to search inside.
But I must return,
to share my roses,
coffee and a chat.
For a resonating vibration,
you give to me,
and I give back.

What I Need

Don't bring me a lemon,
tell me to make lemonade,
that is not all to the recipe.
Likewise, don't label me
this or that,
or anything at all,
I am way more complex,
robust and full of flavour
than any one sentence,
or even two could describe.
But tell me you love me,
I'll be happy with that,
as long as it's true,
and you stick to the fact.

Whatever Life Brings

Bring me the mountain
Bring me the stream
Bring me the cobbled road
Or bring me the dream
I can handle all you bring to me
I thrive, no matter the contours

Clearing the Haze

The past is but a haunted place,
with ghosts I thought I'd buried.
I wish to find the happy things
I've left in perfect positioning,
down this lane of memories.
How do I bust these demons out?
The only way to excise them,
is to walk my way through them.
They'll dissipate once processed,
like the fog they locked me in,
clarity will be found in their release.

Get Out the Way

I promise to step out of the way today,
not hinder nor impede progress,
to shake my head and lose the thought
when it leaps to scornfully condemn.

I promise to be on my best behaviour,
to encourage and motivate,
remind myself of the magnificence within,
to be my own greatest support.

I promise to adopt this outlook henceforth.

Out of Broken

Rain must come from broken clouds,
sometimes lashed from a fractured sky,
eggs from shells that have been cracked,
and mighty trees once broke the soil to grow.
To move beyond the limits of our boxes
ceilings must be shattered to oblivion,
and at times we must splinter and implode,
our hearts and souls dropped glasses,
melted, heated, and life blown anew
from the sharp shards of the old.

Trust It

Indescribable knowing
Without logic and reason
Suspicious sorcery
In the deepest gut sense
Neck hairs at attention
Arm's standing too
Don't doubt the most
Knowing you know
Soul wisdom
It's true

Doing Your Part

Spider, spider
Thy web is spun
Thy work is done
And now in faith
You sit and wait
With belief in place
You wait to eat
For the fly to fall
For a certain feast

Believing in You

Hello beautiful, gorgeous, handsome,
may your day be magical,
and your self-belief infinite.

Let's Take a Look

Come along with you,
to the mirror we go,
let us find all the flaws
you are constantly listing,
every imperfection you know.
Perhaps we could add one or two,
how would that do for you?
Look at you! Just look!
Have you had enough?
Well, I have!
Because I wonder
if you have considered
your most radiant soul.
There is a list as long as my arm,
of wonder and magic and greatness,
that all reside within you.
Stop looking for all that is wrong,
acknowledge the good existing inside.

Little Lights

When sadness eclipses everything
Look for the pinholes of light
Many stars brighten the darkest sky

The Ghost of Me

Ghost asking for permission to be
Standing in the place where I am
Stepping aside for everyone else
You can no longer be a part of me

In the Centre

The centre of everything is nowhere,
for when you think it is found
the world shifts, shapes added,
your calibration begins again.
The centre of the earth is nowhere,
rocks form, crumble, and the axis tilts,
continuously changing and moving,
your calibration begins again.
The centre of this magical existence is
You,
You,
are the centre of this magical existence.
Without arrogance this must be true,
for not, the search for the middle would cease
because we would not be interested to know.
The centre of the earth is each and everyone.
We must be the crucial axis of our world,
each a balanced overlapping mini solar system,
and we must be our own luminescent sun,
for the centre of everything is each and everyone.

Work of art

In the breath I take
The colours I see
Music I hear
This splendid body
In the swirls
Of my fingertips
In each organ that beats
Pulses and vibrates
I am magical energy

Come Out of Hiding

Lift your head magical soul,
the ground has nothing to show you.
Stare life dead in the face,
see the blessings it has to offer,
open your arms magical soul,
the foetal position has nothing to give you,
stretch wide into the chest of life,
embrace the experiences it gives.
Pick up your feet magical soul,
stagnancy has nothing to offer you,
walk towards the gifts of life,
run, dance, and play in exhilaration.

Two Sides of One Line

I sit on the line of yin and yang
Admiring the duality
Without dark, no light
Without hot, no cold
Fabulous balance of all
I see
I experience
Not only good, not only bad
It is the grace of the line I walk
Constantly reminding myself
Should I fall to one side
The glory of the other

Who I Am

Who am I you want to know
I am blood
I am flesh
And I am bone
I am spirit
I am soul
And I am magic
Celestial stardust
Of the Universe
I am a magnificent creation
That is who I am

Who Are You?

Don't tell me you're sorry
Because I don't want to hear
Don't you be apologising to me
For who you are
It isn't necessary
It isn't required
Don't apologise for who you are
Unless you don't want to be
Then it is up to you
To change it
But don't apologise for it

Everyday Best

If today you can only lift your head,
and know within your heart
without doubt, this is your best,
then lift your head as high as you can,
and do it with an attitude of success.
For tomorrow you'll do your best again,
building the foundation each day,
you will come to achieve your utmost.

Extreme Dreaming

Lavender blues and periwinkle pies
These are my dreams up in the sky
Pink, purple shades of possibilities
May they be magic and not inevitabilities
Of hurricanes and tornadoes blown
Of struggles and difficulties in various forms
May I be allowed to immerse myself
In fantasy, more vivid that life
Transmuted to sublime reality
This be my truth by Universal decree

Whisper Your Wishes to the Wind

Bearers of wishes
Fairies and dandelions
Give them to the ether
In detailed form
Have faith in their abilities

Sleeping at Night

Golden sliver of light
Slice me to the bone
Find my intentions
For the glorious day
Magnify their brilliance
In the sparkle of your glow
Let them radiate brightest
In every action I take
Until they meet the milky moon
And twinkling stars
Let these goals sleep
Until tomorrow
When we will happily
continue again

The Way Out

I do not know what I need to hear today
In these doldrums where my soul and I lay
But the Universe will softly whisper it my way
No coincidental conversations would say
All planned in serendipitous time delay
We shall find the exit out of this dismay.

Come See

I'll lift you to the mirror to see
The wonder I do
In the hopes you will believe
That it is you

Life's Balance

Life is not filled with feathers and dandelions
It is not whispered so gentle and kind
You must pay exceptional attention
Believe in magnificent possibilities
To be allowed to bear witness to her softer side
And in this faith of magic and miracles
With the expectation of seeing greatness
You may experience the spectacular wonders
The Universe has waiting for us

Standing Straight

Victory is mine when I get out of bed
Victory is mine when I raise my head
You might think this is not enough
But who are you to say just how tough
These little things are for me right now
Walking straight, without a curved bow
Monumental tasks on one given day
I'll celebrate doing it my way

Blessings Deserved

Dear Heart,

Who told you that you were undeserving
of life's greatest gifts,
not enough to receive the best?
When did you start to believe
wonderful things were never meant
to be yours at all?
Is there a quest to become worthy?
Where did this false idea come from?
Because I want to set the record straight:
You are absolutely deserving
to thrive and be blessed
with all that is fantastic and great,
so I ask you please, please,
set the lie that you have ingrained
deeply into your mind, adrift.
To leave your space forever
and allow the glorious in.

My Place of Peace

Give me a great big tree to wrap my arms around
Green grass to feel against the soles of my feet
The sound of crystal running water in a stream
Fresh smell of wildflowers and falling leaves
And let the birds sing my restful melody of peace
Against nature's breast, let me contentedly sleep

Falling

Shoot it to the galaxy
This wild heart of mine
Where no mobile signal will reach
With absolutely no distractions
That it may love the silence
Revel in awe of the stunning splendour
Bask in a million light-year glow
And fall deeply and madly
In love with itself

I Have Today

Mixed emotions in these troubled times,
longings for the years gone by.
Was it they were simpler,
or I younger, with less responsibility?
Was it they were honest,
or I just filled with naivety?
On closer inspection of those memories,
they do not hold up to the canvas of my mind,
they have not stood the test of time.
Perhaps they were not the good old days,
perhaps the best I have is today.
It holds a future I can shape.
I have no sway over the yesterdays,
but the hours from waking 'til sleep
of the day before me, is mine to mould.

Expanding Worth

(Shaped Poem)

The battle
between worth,
birth, and girth,
a searching for reason
of your value to this earth,
sadly non-existent, other than
a false belief in your dearth,
that achingly denies you of your
life's wholly intended, glorious mirth.
But now is the time to dock in your berth,
surrender the fight, in recognition of your innate
importance to this wondrous Earth.

Unknown Name

Not meant to be a quiet mouse
melted into the shadows,
but to be seen and acknowledged.
Not meant to fade into the wallpaper,
into the annuls of obscurity,
but to shine like a celestial body,
warming people's lives.

So What?

I'm so afraid of making a mistake
I don't do anything at all,
excuse my time and procrastinate,
busy, busy, every moment,
with absolutely nothing at all.
I'm standing in the same place
as the year before, and the one
prior to that, fooling no one,
least of all myself.
How big an error could I make?
How extensive the consequences?
How bad would it be?
Fear taunts with a negative response,
but this is my realised reply,
"So what? I'd be moving."

Not On the Surface

(Shaped Poem)

Red rivers of clay and turquoise oceans,
beneath azure skies, or storms of grey.
Complex desert oases and golden sands,
emerald lawns and forests of autumn,
some harsh and unforgiving, others,
soft, puffy clouds of welcoming.
Is she not gorgeous?
Judgement on Nature and
her appearance, subjective
on preference, or the day.
But what of her being
and all that she is, in
self-repair, and giving?
Food for nourishment, and
for great thought, gems for
our wealth, and stones for
our homes, wood for our fires,
and water for our thirst.
Is she not gorgeous?
Who are we to declare truth?
Beneath our skins,
is where you
shall find
us.

Chimera – the Illusion

Envy be thy crooked eye
I am the charlatan of perfection
You have missed naught
In your false misperception
Of lagging in this race
That none can truly win or lose
For my secret lacking
You are in the process
Of rightfully attaining such
Tomorrow you shall be through
And I still pretending
A forgery of triumph

Even in the Crazy

The world may have gone crazy
But the Earth still turns
The sun will rise and light the darkness
The world may have gone crazy
But you are still reading this verse
There is hope for us

Bright Sunflower

In a field of sunflowers
I could not find you
For you are the light
Radiant bright soul
Do not bow your head
To conceal your place
Do not bow your head
To dim for the world
Shine radiant soul
Shine

What's Here, Now?

Seven days before you,
seven days behind you,
How many weeks have you lived?
How many have you existed,
and how many,
have you simply endured?
There is more to this!
Dancing in the kitchen with no music at all,
singing in the shower to the water drops.
Listen to the melody, see the glowing dawn,
hear the birdsong... and breathe.
Don't fight for the air,
let it come naturally.
Let everything simply be,
here,
now,
come back to today.
Don't wander in yesterday's problems,
or wonder in tomorrow's troubles,
because they aren't there,
unless you create them.

Give the Freedom

Don't do it for them to love you,
allow them to, without action nor expectation,
do it because you want to.
Don't turn to see who is watching,
carry on regardless of the audience,
according to your wishes and desires.
Let them love the real and authentic,
give them that choice,
and yourself the freedom to be,
phenomenally you.

What to Do with Dreams

I wake from floating in the sky,
sliding down golden moonbeams,
dancing in glorious starlight,
where impossible is not a word,
and my heart is happy.
Remember the messages
from my slumber,
and proceed to this blank day,
to prove my belief
in all those magical,
imagined dreams.

Celebrate the Wins

The flower in the weeds
fighting to be seen,
stolen worth
clawing to be found,
in the chest
where it's always been.
Unexpected treasure
waiting like a seed,
for the surface to be cracked,
to push and struggle
into brilliant light.
Let us cheer in support,
for the victory in this fight,
but know there will be more,
all in strength and growth
for future use.

Kama' Aina

(Just one of those words I love)

Feet in the sand
Child of the land
The belonging soul
Making it whole
Together done
World as one

KEEP BALANCING

About the Author

Debbie Gravett will make you stop the car to photograph a beautiful tree; just ask her husband and two daughters. Living in South Africa gives her magnificent landscapes, wildlife, and coastlines with crashing waves from which to draw energy and peace.

She has written a poetry blog for more than a decade, and her flash fiction has appeared in the anthologies *City in a Wild Garden: Stories of the Nature of Cities, Vol. 2* (2021) and *Bolts of Fiction* (2024).

Debbie writes to understand life and shares it to touch reader's souls, offering encouragement, hoping they will feel seen, heard, less alone, and motivated to keep going. She believes in magic, dreams, kindness, and lifting one another up—one sentence at a time.

If you enjoyed this book, please tell others about it.

www.debbiegravett.co.za

www.ingramcontent.com/pod-product-compliance
Lightning Source LLC
LaVergne TN
LVHW091131080826
845145LV00008B/2117

* 9 7 8 1 0 4 9 2 5 2 5 3 7 *